1 *Charles Genuys, frontispiece to article by Genuys in* Revue des Arts Décoratifs, *1895*

LA RECHERCHE DU STYLE NOUVEAU

2 *Alphonse Mucha, cover of* L'Image, *December 1896*

LE PAPIER PEINT

À L'EXPOSITION UNIVERSELLE DE 1900

'ÉTUDE du papier peint à l'Exposition universelle de 1900 présente un intérêt tout exceptionnel, non seulement parce qu'on retrouve dans les spécimens offerts à notre appréciation des qualités d'exécution fort remarquables, non seulement parce que les progrès mécaniques réalisés depuis vingt ans ont permis d'atteindre, dans la fabrication à la machine, une perfection presque égale à ce qu'on obtenait jadis avec les procédés d'impression à la planche, si longs et si coûteux, mais parce que le parti pris général des dessins, le choix et l'arrangement des sujets, les harmonies cherchées dans les tonalités assoupies auxquelles on donne aujourd'hui la préférence, semblent annoncer que la décoration ordinaire de nos logis est à la veille de subir une transformation à peu près radicale. Ceci demande quelques explications.

Les lecteurs habituels de cette *Revue* constituent un public trop renseigné, trop avisé, familiarisé de trop longue date avec tout ce qui regarde la parure de nos habitations, pour que nous ayons la téméraire pensée de lui apprendre une chose nouvelle, en constatant qu'il existe deux manières de décorer nos appartements. Ces deux modes différents, ces deux partis très distincts, qui, sans s'exclure absolument, ont

3 *Grégoire,* Illumination *(engraved by Rousset), for an article on wallpaper designs exhibited in the 1900 exhibition in* Revue des Arts Décoratifs, *Vol. XX, 1900*

4 *Title page of* The Cabinet Maker and Art Furnisher, *September 1900*

5 *Louis Majorelle, chair (detail of back) exhibited in the 1900 Exhibition, cf. Fig. 4 (Bethnal Green Museum)*

The Decoration of the Suburban House

WINDOW WITH ORNAMENTED SHUTTERS   BY M. H. B. SCOTT

If paper is used, a design which should suggest, without imitating, panelling on the same lines as the canopy work in stained-glass windows, would are casements opening outwards, and carefully designed to secure in the most exposed situations perfect freedom from draughts.

6 *Woodcut illustrating a decorative scheme by M. H. Baillie Scott for an imaginary suburban house,* The Studio, *Vol. V, 1894*

7 *Half-tone photographic reproduction of watercolour sketch by M. H. Baillie Scott, of the garden front of a projected 'Country House', The Studio, Vol. XIX, 1900*

8 *Wood engraving of garden front of 'Walnut Tree Farm', by C. F. A. Voysey, The Studio, Vol. XI, 1897*

A COUNTRY HOUSE · M. H. BAILLIE SCOTT, ARCHITECT

THE GARDEN FRONT, WALNUT TREE FARM · C. F. A. VOYSEY, ARCHITECT

Intérieur de Salon.

Intérieur · T. HERBERT ET FRANCES McNAIR

9 *Photograph, reproduced in half-tone, of room by G. Serrurier-Bovy in the Hotel Chatham, in Art et Décoration, Vol. XII, 1902*

10 *Photograph, reproduced in half-tone, of room exhibited by T. Herbert and Frances McNair at the Turin Exhibition, 1902, in Art et Décoration, Vol. XII, 1902*

11 *Bruno Paul, page layout designed as a setting for a poem by Victor Hardung, 'Seelen' ('Souls') in* Jugend (Youth) *Vol. II, 1896*

12 *Otto Eckmann, illumination and setting of a poem by Karl Henckell, in* Pan, *Vol. II, 1895–6*

13 *Otto Eckmann, electric lamp, exhibited in Munich Kunstausstellung, photograph printed in half-tone in* Dekorative Kunst, *Vol. I, 1897*

14 *Joseph Maria Olbrich, setting of a poem by Rilke, from* Advent, *reprinted in* Ver Sacrum, *September 1898*

Ein Händeineinanderlegen,
Ein langer Kuss auf kühlen Mund,
Und dann: auf schimmerweissen Wegen
Durchwandern wir den Wiesengrund.

Durch leisen, weissen Blütenregen
Schickt uns der Tag den ersten Kuss —
Mir ist: Wir wandeln Gott entgegen,
Der durchs Gebreite kommen muss.
                    RAINER MARIA RILKE.

15 *Olbrich, architectural sketch, in* Ver Sacrum, *July* 1898

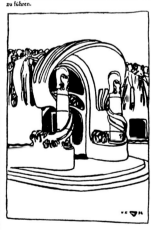

VER SACRUM

Zimmern ein ausgesucht interessantes Bild der Aussenwelt erhält; man wird es dann nicht mehr verstehen, dass man einst die durchsichtigen Fensterscheiben ohne Wahl überall anbrachte.

Es gibt also ein Radicalmittel, das ein neues Haus unter allen Umständen aus dem Schablonencharakter herausheben muss: man bringe nur Licht und Luft auf verschiedenen Wegen ins Haus — und die ästhetische Wirkung wird nicht ausbleiben.

Man schaffe die durchsichtigen Fenster mindestens zur Hälfte ab und ersetze das Öffnen der Fenster durch Luft-Accumulatoren.

Selbstverständlich kann eigentlich nur das freistehende, nach allen Seiten gegliederte Einzelhaus einen Anspruch auf architektonischen Wert erheben. Aber auch das Grossstadthaus könnte durch eine Revolution im Fensterarrangement ein künstlerisches Ansehen bekommen.

Jedenfalls müsste es bei allen Neubauten modern werden, Licht und Luft auf verschiedenen Wegen ins Haus zu führen.

STUDIEN ZUR DECORATIVEN AUSGESTALTUNG EINES HAUSEINGANGES VON JOSEF HOFFMANN.

Buchschmuck für V.S gez. v. J. M. Olbrich.

Die Wiener Gewerbetreibenden werden das nicht sobald einsehen. Erst bis auch bei uns der Dilettantismus eine Macht geworden sein wird, erst bis dadurch das allgemeine Niveau der künstlerischen Bildung sich gehoben hat, erst bis das Publicum selbst in peremptorischer Weise dem Kunsthandwerk höhere Aufgaben stellen wird, dann erst dürften unsere „Abderiten" ihren Widerstand aufgeben.

Aus der Familie, aus dem Hause muss die Regeneration des Kunstgewerbes ausgehen. Wir müssen Menschen erziehen, die ein unpersönliches, kahles Zimmer unerträglich finden, denen schlechtgestimmte Farben, hässliche Proportionen direct körperliches Unbehagen verursachen. Sie werden dann — besonders die Frauen mit ihrem ebenso ästhetischen als praktischen Sinn — Forderungen stellen, aus denen sich der wirklich künstlerische Gebrauchsgegenstand entwickeln wird. Billig, logisch und dem Auge gefällig.

Denn vorläufig ist das Kunstgewerbe noch zu sehr Zier. Es muss erst urwüchsiger werden durch die tägliche Gemeinschaft — in der Familie. B. ZUCKERKANDL

Entwurf von J. M. Olbrich.

EINFACHE MÖBEL

16 *Josef Hoffmann, architectural sketches accompanying an article by Paul Scheerbart, 'Licht und Luft' ('Light and Air'), in* Ver Sacrum, *July* 1898

17 *Joseph Maria Olbrich, page of illustrations including his own designs for 'simple furniture',* Ver Sacrum, *July* 1898

1 *Casa Battló, façade remodelled by Gaudí, 1905–7*

2 *Casa Vicens, 1878–80 (enlarged 1925–6 under Gaudí's supervision)*

3 *Casa Vicens, detail of street façade*

4 *Park Güell, tilework on part of the monumental steps, 1900–14*

5 *Casa Vicens, railing in cast iron and steel supports 1878–80*

7 *Chair designed for the Casa Calvet, c. 1901*

6 *Finca Güell, entrance and gate, 1887*

8 *Seat on the raised terrace (intended as an open air theatre), Park Güell, 1900–14*

10 *Park Güell, plan*

9 *Raised terrace, Park Güell, 1900–14*

11 *Park Güell, terracing 'Palm Tree' buttresses, 1900–14*

12 *Park Güell, terracing buttresses, 1900–14*

13 *Park Güell, Doric columns supporting the raised terrace (see Fig. 9), 1900–14*

14 *Chapel for Colonia Güell (only lower portion completed) at Santa Coloma de Cervello, 1898–1915*

15 *Chapel for Colonia Güell, area under the main stairs, at entrance to the crypt, 1898–1915*

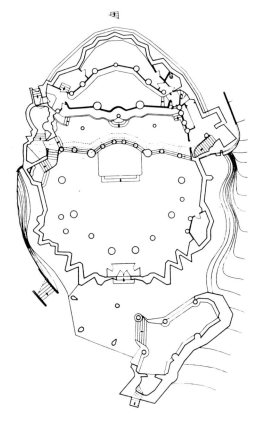

17 *Chapel for Colonia Güell, plan of crypt*

16 *Chapel for Colonia Güell, vaulting*

Expiatory Church of the Sagrada Familia (Holy Family), transept façade of the Nativity seen from inside the unfinished nave. Part of the Neo-Gothic apse can be seen on the left (finished 1893). The lower parts of the transept façade begun in the 1890s, the naturalistic sculpture is from around 1903–10, the towers around 1920, the spires completed 1927–30

18

Funicular model of the Chapel for the Colonia Güell, 1898–1900. Gaudí actually designed the internal and external façades of the Chapel tracing over photographs of these models.

20

19 *Sagrada Familia, 'Nativity' façade, external face, with naturalistic sculpture, c. 1903–10*

21 *Large scale model of the nave for the Sagrada Familia based on the one Gaudí was working on between 1925 and his death*

22 *Casa Milá, 1905–10, first floor plan*

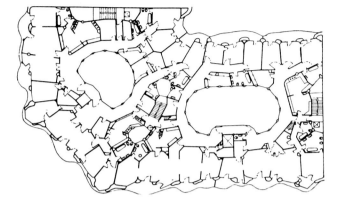

24 *Casa Milá, view of street front*

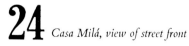

23, a. b: *Casa Milá, views of street front*

25 *Casa Milá, view into the main courtyard, from the entrance*

1 *Hector Guimard, Castel Henriette, Sèvres, begun 1899 (demolished 1969)*

2 *Hector Guimard, Castel Henriette, plan of ground floor (Note the changes in the completed building, Fig 1)*

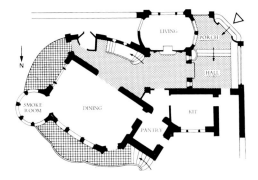

3 *Hector Guimard, Castel Henriette, dining room*

5 *Hector Guimard, Villa Flore, dining room*

6 *Hector Guimard, Villa Flore, plan of first floor*

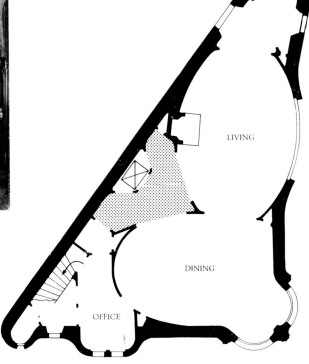

4 *Hector Guimard, Villa Flore, 122 avenue Mozart, Paris, begun 1909*

7 *Hector Guimard, cast-iron balcony grill*

8 *Hector Guimard, Villa Jassedé, 41 rue Chardon-Lagache, Paris, begun 1893*

8a *Villa Jassedé, detail*

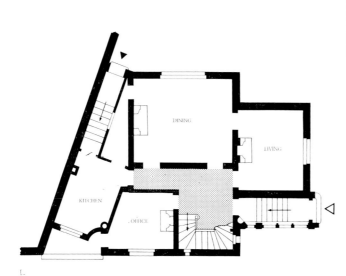

9 *Hector Guimard, Villa Jassedé, plan of first floor*

10 *Hector Guimard, Villa Jassedé, ceramics framing window on upper storey*

11 *Hector Guimard, Sacré Coeur School, 9 avenue de la Frillière, Paris, begun 1895*

12 *E.-E. Viollet-le-Duc, Plate 21 from* Entretiens sur l'architecture *(Paris) 1864*

13 *Hector Guimard, Sacré Coeur school, details*

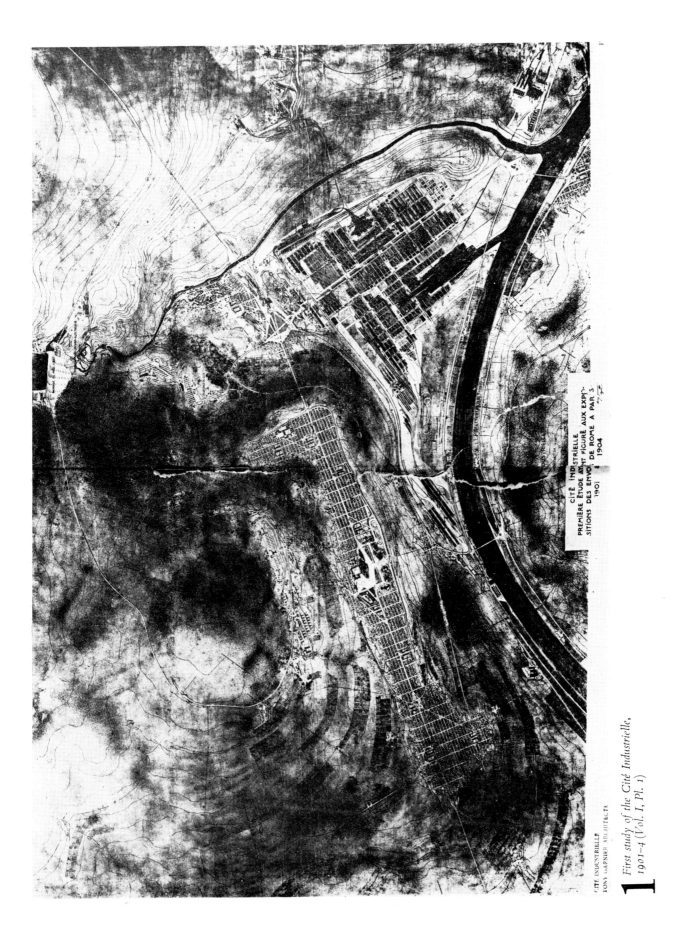

1 *First study of the Cité Industrielle, 1901–4 (Vol. I, Pl. 1)*

Note:
All illustrations (except Fig. 6a) are from the first edition of Garnier's *Cité Industrielle*, published in 2 volumes, Paris, 1917

2 *Railway station concourse (Vol. I, Pl. 64)*

3 *Central administrative building, portico (Vol. I, Pl. 17)*

4 *Heliotherapeutic centre (Vol. 1, Pl. 58)*

5 *Residential quarter (Vol. 2, Pl. 5)*

6 *Art school, main hall (Vol. 1, Pl. 43)*

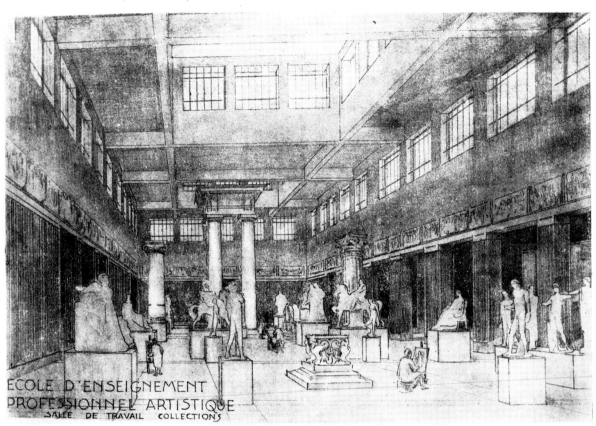

6a *Ecole des Beaux-Arts, Paris main hall*

7 *'Atrium' of private house (Vol. 2, Pl. 128)*

8 *Perspective of Cité Industrielle, showing environs, 1917 (Vol. 2, Pl. 76)*

9 *Residential quarter, view (Vol. 2, Pl. 132)*

10 *Hall for temporary exhibitions (Vol. 1, Pl. 24)*

11 *Assembly hall and clock tower (Vol. 1, Pl. 15)*

12 *Power station and furnaces (Vol. 2, Pl. 164)*

Figures 9–12 are not referred to during the programme

1 *The Hennebique system (patented 1892)*

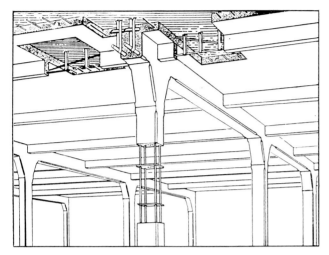

2 *François Hennebique, villa, rue du Lycée Lakanal, Bourg-La-Reine, begun 1904*

3 *François Hennebique, villa, Bourg-La-Reine, water tower*

4 *François Hennebique, villa, Bourg-La-Reine, roof terrace*

5 *C. Klein, apartments, 9 Rue Claude-Chahu, Passy, 1903 (using the Hennebique system)*

6 *Auguste Perret, apartments, 25 bis Rue Franklin, Paris, 1902*

7 *Auguste Perret, apartments, 25 bis Rue Franklin, Paris, 1902*

8 *Auguste Perret, Notre Dame du Raincy, Le Raincy, 1924, interior*

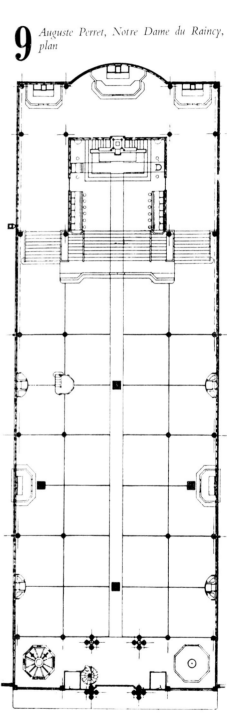

9 *Auguste Perret, Notre Dame du Raincy, plan*

10 *Auguste Perret, Notre Dame du Raincy, view across nave*

11 *Auguste Perret, Notre Dame du Raincy, main façade*

12 *Auguste Perret, Notre Dame du Raincy (showing exterior of cupola)*

13 *Auguste Perret, Notre Dame du Raincy (interior of cupola)*

12a *(above centre) Auguste Perret, Notre Dame du Raincy, detail of glass wall in South flank*

14 *Auguste Perret, Mobilier National, Paris, 1935, plan, ground floor*

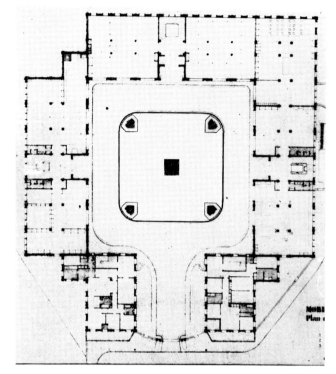

15 *Auguste Perret, Mobilier National, main entrance*

16 *Auguste Perret, Mobilier National (view to right from entrance)*

17 *Auguste Perret, Mobilier National, detail of south-west façade*

1 *Louis Sullivan, Wainwright building, St Louis, 1890–1*

2 *Louis Sullivan, Guaranty Building, Buffalo, 1894–5*

3 *Louis Sullivan, Gage Building, Chicago, 1898–9 (with buildings by Holabird and Roche, 1898–9, on left)*

9 *Louis Sullivan, Plate 2 from Louis Sullivan,* A System of Architectural Ornament according with a Philosophy of Man's Powers, *1924*

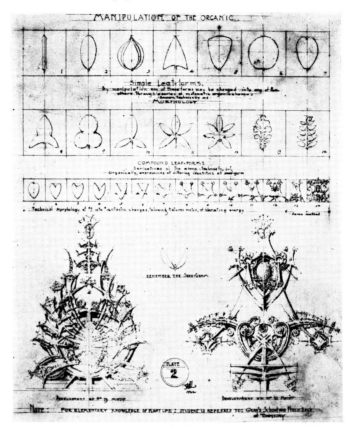

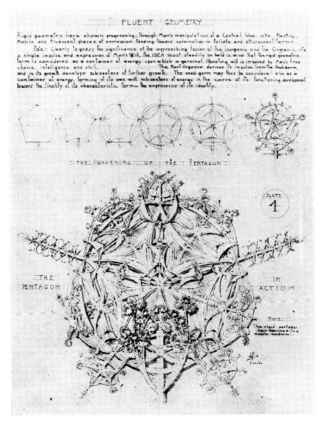

10 *Louis Sullivan, Plate 4 from Louis Sullivan,* A System of Architectural Ornament according with a Philosophy of Man's Powers, *1924*

1 *Umberto Boccioni, 'The Noise of the Street Enters the House', 1911 (Niedersächsische Landesgalerie, Hanover)*

2 *Antonio Sant'Elia, Power Station 1914, coloured inks, 31 × 20.5 cm (coll. Paride Accetti, Milan)*

3 *Antonio Sant'Elia, Central Station, 1912(?) Note the various traffic levels and interchanges. The sketch may be connected with Sant'Elia's work for the Milan station competition, but seems more likely to be an inspired later development of the same theme*

4 *Antonio Sant'Elia, Città Nuova drawing, 1914, ink and pencil, 52.5 × 51.5 cm (coll. Sant'Elia, Villa Communale dell'Olmo, Como). One of the few definitely attributable drawings of the Città Nuova group exhibited at the Nuove Tendenze exhibition in 1914. Note once more the various traffic levels and the detached lift shafts linked by galleries to the stepped-back façade of the apartment block.*

5 *Antonio Sant'Elia, apartment block with step-backs, 1914, ink, pencil and watercolour, 27.5 × 11.5 cm (coll. Paride Accetti, Milan)*

6 *Josef Plečnik, sketch, 1899. Quite close parallels can be found between Sant'Elia's early work and that of the Viennese Wagnerschule architects such as Plečnik and Emil Hoppe*

8 *Antonio Sant'Elia, project for Milan Station, 1912 (from a contemporary photograph in the possession of the Sant'Elia family). Drawing made by Sant'Elia on behalf of Cantoni for the competition for a new station for Milan*

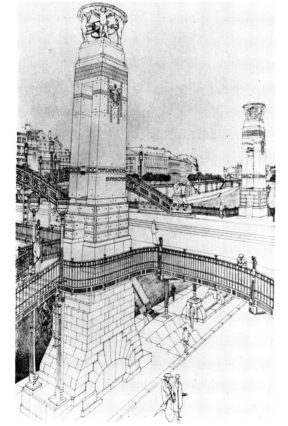

7 *Otto Wagner, design for the Ferdinand bridge in Vienna, 1905*

10 *Antonio Sant'Elia, power station, 1914, pencil, ink and watercolour, 30 × 20 cm (coll. Accide Paretti, Milan)*

9 *Antonio Sant'Elia, Central Station, 1914, ink and crayon, 50 × 39 cm (coll. Sant'Elia, Villa Communale dell'Olmo, Como). One of the Città Nuova drawings exhibited in 1914*

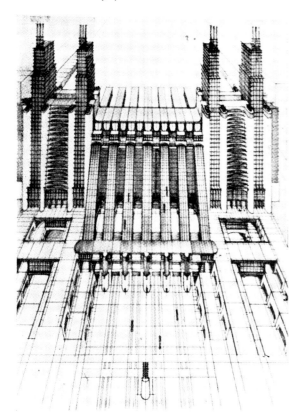

11 *Grain silo, Buffalo, from* Jahrbuch des Deutschen Werkbundes, *1913*

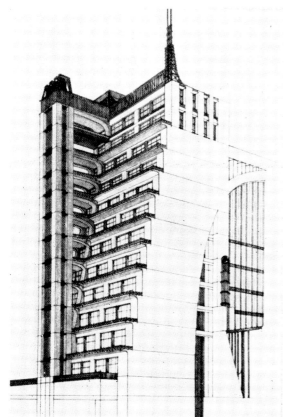

12 *Antonio Sant'Elia, apartment block with step-backs, 1914, ink and crayon, 38.5 × 24 cm (coll. Sant'Elia, Villa Communale dell'Olmo, Como). Note the illuminated advertising sign incorporated at roof level.*

13 *Henri Sauvage, apartment block, 26 rue Vavin, Paris, 1912*

14 *Frans Masereel, drawing from Die Stadt (The City), first published Berlin, 1925*

6 N
el

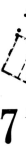

7

2 *L. A., V. A. and A. A. Vesnin, competition project for the Palace of Labour, Moscow, 1922–3, perspective view. (The project won third prize in the competition.)*

1 *B. M. Iofan and V. Gelfreikh, project for the Palace of Soviets, Moscow, 1934 version*

9 *Le Corbusier, project for the Centrosoyus headquarters in Moscow 1928/9, bird's eye view*

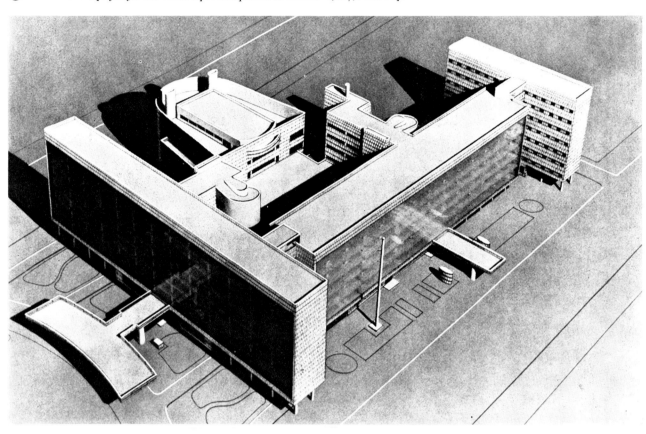

NEUTRALISING walls of glass or stone. Hermetically sealed system of circulating dry air. Hot (winter), cold (summer).

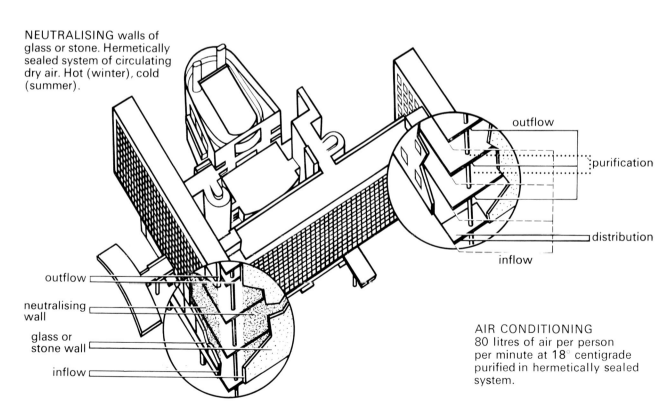

outflow

purification

distribution

inflow

outflow

neutralising wall

glass or stone wall

inflow

AIR CONDITIONING
80 litres of air per person per minute at 18° centigrade purified in hermetically sealed system.

10 *Le Corbusier, project for the Centrosoyus headquarters in Moscow, 1928/9. Bird's eye view with cutaway to show the system of air conditioning and the 'neutralizing wall'*

11 *Sass (Sector of Architects of Socialist Construction) competition project for the Palace of Soviets, Moscow, 1931–2, section*

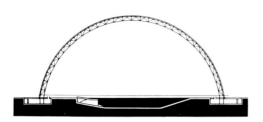

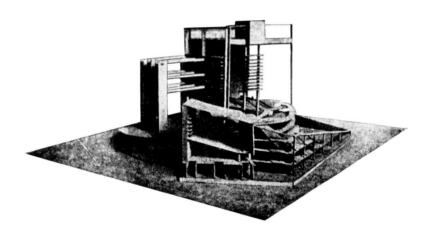

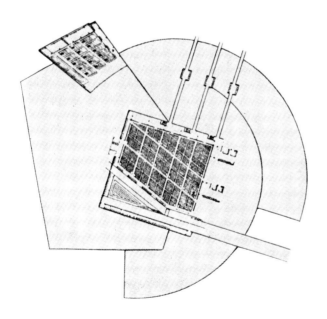

12 *Asnova (Association of Contemporary Architects), competition project for the Palace of Soviets, Moscow, 1931–2. Top: model. Bottom: plan*

6 Secti
brick
parti

Note

9 *Pierre Chareau, model of the Maison de Verre, exhibited in 1931*

10 *Perspective sketch of the Salon from one end of the glass wall, 1929–31*

11 *Construction photo of the Maison de Verre half-finished, (1931)*

12 *View down from the gallery to where the main stairs will go (1930)*

13 *View of main salon (1931)*

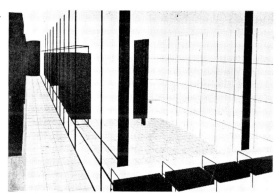

14 *Perspective sketch of the Salon and gallery, taken from the gallery 1929-31*

15 *A portion of the Nevada glass tile wall in Dr Dalsace's office (1930)*

16 *Photograph (1933) showing the main salon from the gallery*

17 *Photograph (recent) showing the main salon*

18 *The main staircase (1933)*

19 *The pivoting mesh screens at the foot of the main staircase, ground floor (1933)*

20 *Foot of main staircase, ground floor (1933)*

21 *The main staircase leading up from the first to the second floor (1933)*

22 *Detail of materials on the sliding screens in the main salon (1933)*

23 *The duralumin cupboards in the bathroom (1933)*

24 *(left) view from the small salon towards the extending ladder leading to the master bedroom (1933)*

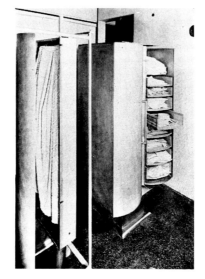

25 *Washing unit in one of the subsidiary bedrooms (1933)*

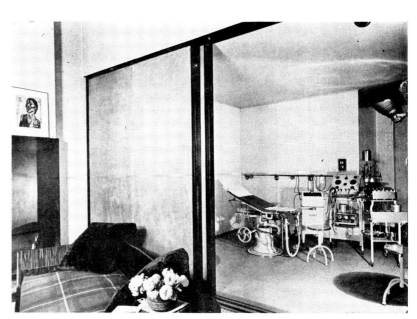

26 *The main façade lit by the external floodlights at night (1933)*

27 *View from Dr Dalsace's office to the consulting room (1933)*

1 *Walter Gropius and Marcel Breuer, Werkbund exhibit, Salon des Artistes Décorateurs, Paris, 1930*

2 *Charlotte Perriand, dining room exhibited at the Salon d'Automne, Paris, 1928*

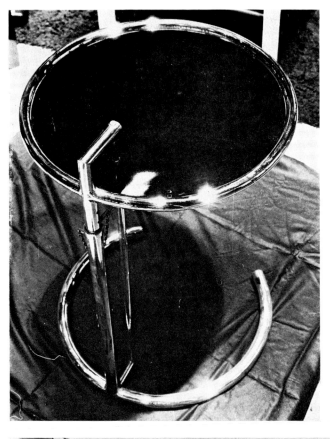

3 *Eileen Gray, small table, c. 1928, chromed metal support and lacquered metal top*

4 *Jean Dunand, 'fumoir' (smoking room), designed for the French Embassy exhibited by the Société des Artistes Décorateurs, Exposition Internationale des Arts Décoratifs, Paris, 1925*

5 Marcel Coard, *chest of drawers, veneer, with panels of pearl and lapis lazuli (private collection, Paris)*

6 Jean Dunand, *occasional table c. 1923, beaten copper with silver inlay (private collection, Paris)*

7 Jean Dunand, *'coiffeuse', amber coloured lacquer, exhibited in the Salon des Artistes Décorateurs, Paris, 1930 (private collection, Paris)*

8 Jean Dunand, *'coiffeuse', amber coloured lacquer, exhibited in the Salon des Artistes Décorateurs, Paris, 1930 (private collection, Paris)*

1 *Cabinet by Gordon Russell (made by William Marks) of walnut inlaid with ebony, box and laburnum, 1924 (Gold Medal at Paris Exhibition, 1925)*

2 *Oval double gate leg dining table by Gordon Russell, in English oak, 1926*

3 *Detail of base of gate legs, showing dowel hinges and wedged dovetails in the rails*

4 *Detail of dovetails in map chest (cf. Fig. 5)*

5 *Map chest, by Gordon Russell, in oak, numbered to store Gordon Russell plans*

6 *Detail of upper part of Figure 1, showing brass hinges and drawers inlaid with ebony, box edges and laburnum 'oysters'*

7 *Detail of Figure 1, showing dovetails of drawers and top edge of carcase*

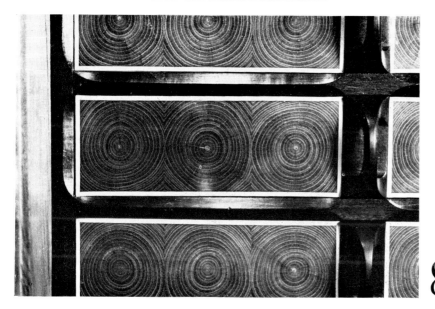

8 *Detail of Figure 1, showing laburnum 'oysters', box edging and ebony framing members*

17 *Detail of Figure 18, showing cross-banded veneering on front edge, and dovetailing and veneering of paper drawer*

19 *Detail of Figure 18, showing the way the veneer is continued from the top to the sides, and broken deliberately on either side of the central section*

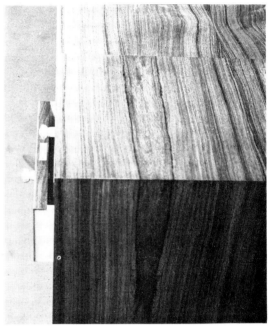

18 *Desk by Eden Minns, veneered in Brazilian rosewood and box, 1930*

NB   All the pieces illustrated, except Figs. 13 and 14, were manufactured and sold by Gordon Russell Limited.

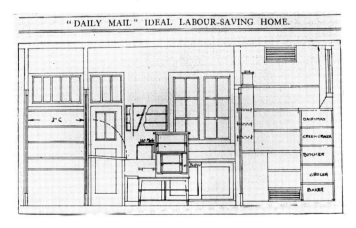

1 *Kitchen with coal range and gas lighting*

2 *Competition design for the Daily Mail 'Labour Saving House' competition, 1920*

3 *Elevation of kitchen in Fig. 2*

4 *Battersea Electric House, 1927, hall (part of electricity showrooms built by the Borough of Battersea)*

5 *Living room*

6 *Dining room*

7 *Bedroom*

8 *Battersea Electric House, 1927, Bathroom*

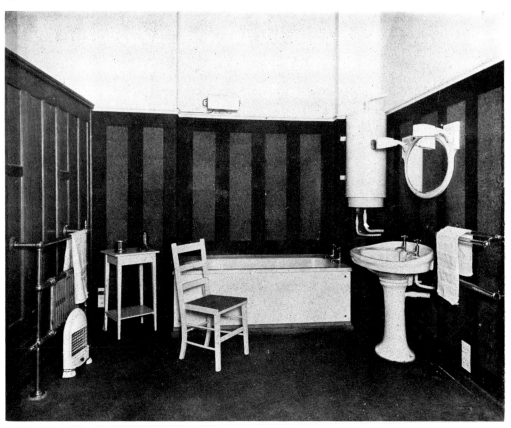

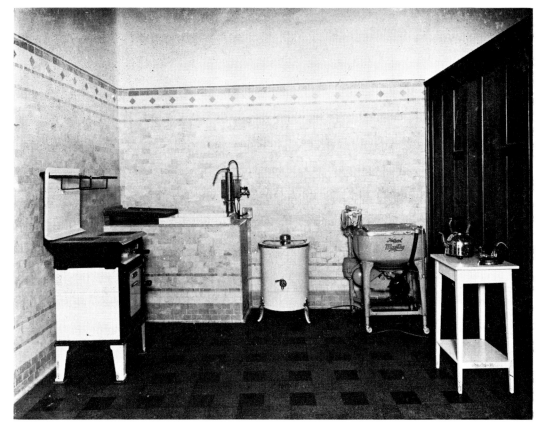

9 *Kitchen*

10 *Kitchen-scullery of 'Wickham', Four Oaks, near Sutton Coldfield, c. 1920*

11 *Kitchen, c. 1920*

 *Typical kitchen in suburban house of the 1920s*

 *Small kitchen, c. 1936*

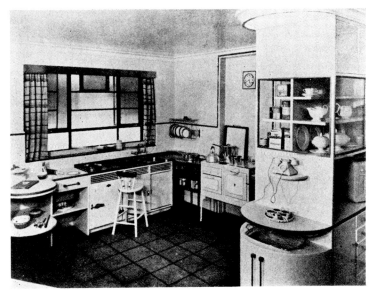 *Kitchen designed by Mrs Darcy Bradell, 1937*

(a) *Alvar Aalto, cellulose factory, Sunila, Finland, 1936–9*

(b) *Workers' housing, Sunila, Finland, 1936–9*

(c) *Workers' housing, Kauttua, Finland, 1938–9*

(d) *Villa Mairea, Noormarkku, Finland, 1938–9*

(e) *Villa Mairea, Norrmarkku, Finland, 1938–9*

(g) *National Pensions Institute, Helsinki, Finland, 1952–6*

(h) *National Pensions Institute, Helsinki, Finland, 1952–6, interior*

(f) *Town Hall, Säynätsalto, Finland, 1950–52*

These illustrations are not mentioned in the programme.
They are intended to provide a summary of Aalto's later development.

1 *Alvar Aalto, Sanatorium, Paimio, Finland, 1929–30, plan*
Key: (A) Patients' wing and sun terraces (B) communal block (C) Service wing (D) Garages (E) Housing for doctors (F) Housing for other employees

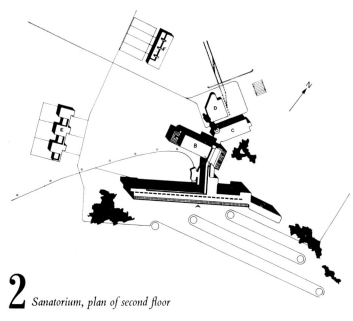

4 *Patients' wing*

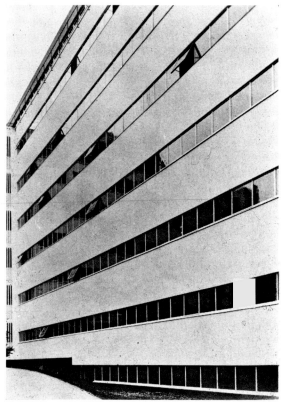

2 *Sanatorium, plan of second floor*

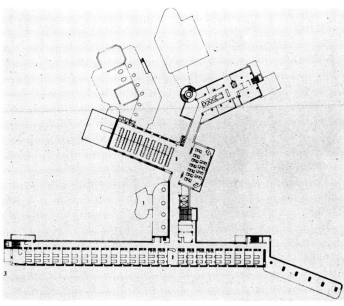

3 *View from the west (patients' wing on right)*

5 *East elevation (with the communal block on right)*

6 *View from the east (with sun terraces on left)*

9 *South elevation of patients' wing*

7 *Detail of sun terraces from south east*

10 *View along roof terraces of patients' wing*

8 *Section through sun terraces*

11 *View from the west*

12 *Plan of typical patient's room*

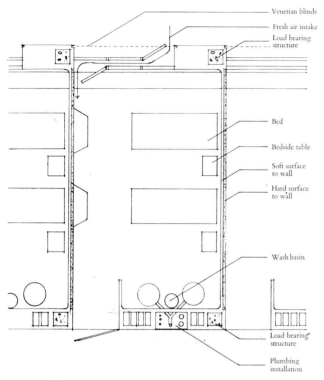

Venetian blinds
Fresh air intake
Load bearing structure
Bed
Bedside table
Soft surface to wall
Hard surface to wall
Wash basin
Load bearing structure
Plumbing installation

14 *Specially designed hand basin (the angle at which water comes out of the taps reduces splashing and noise)*

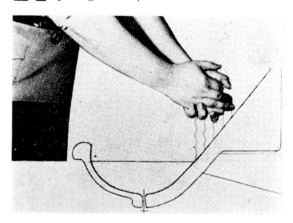

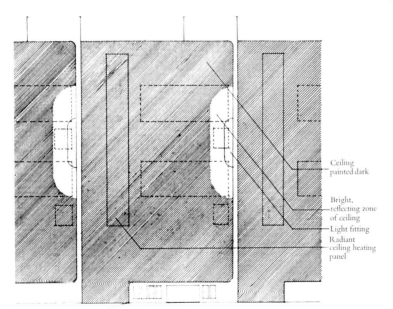

Ceiling painted dark
Bright, reflecting zone of ceiling
Light fitting
Radiant ceiling heating panel

13 *Radiant heating ceiling panel in patient's room*

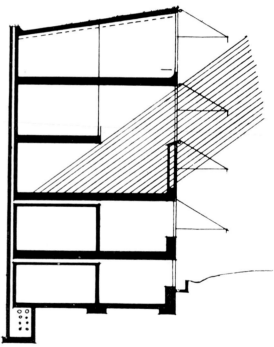

15 *Section through the communal block (dining room is in centre), showing evening light*

16 *Dining room*

17 *Entrance foyer*

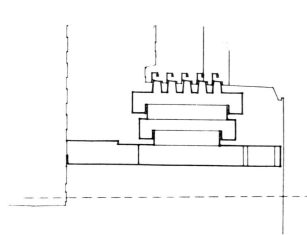

18 *Alvar Aalto, Iron Federation Building, Helsinki, section through skylights*

20 *Kitchens*

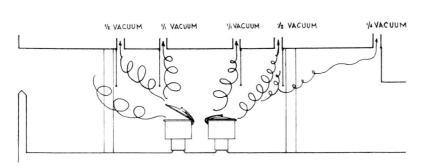

19 *Diagram of ventilation system in the kitchens of the Sanatorium, Paimio*

21 *Typical patients' room*

22 *Corridor*

23 *Traditional Finnish farmhouse, Murtovaara*

24 *Traditional Finnish farmhouse, Murtovaara*

26 *Gesellius, Lindgren and Saarinen, artists' colony, Hvitträsk, Finland, 1902*

25 *Gesellius, Lindgren and Saarinen, artists' colony, Hvitträsk*

1 *Werner March, Reichsbanksiedlung, Berlin-Schmargendorf, 1926*

2 *Walter Gropius, The Bauhaus, Dessau, 1925–6 (left, Trade School and administrative office; right, workshops)*

3 Paul Schmitthenner, Germanic House, Stuttgart, 1924–5
(Page from Wasmuths Monatshefte, 1926)

4 *Bruno Taut, Onkel Toms Hutte Siedlung, Berlin-Zehlendorf, begun 1926. Corner facing Fischtal Siedlung*

5 *Fritz Schopohl, housing in Fischtal Siedlung, Berlin-Zehlendorf, 1928*

7 *Heinrich Tessenow, house in Fischtal Siedlung, Berlin-Zehlendorf, 1928*

6 *Paul Schmitthenner, house in Fischtal Siedlung, Berlin-Zehlendorf, 1928*

8 *Hermann Muthesius, Haus von Velsen, Berlin-Zehlendorf, 1926*

8a *Plan*

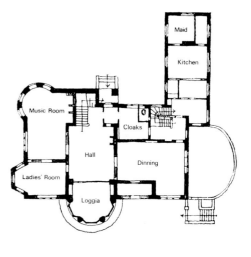

9 *Friedrich Ostendorf, Muthesius's Haus von Velsen redesigned*

9a *Plan*

10 *Heinrich Tessenow, design for a small terrace house, c. 1916, garden front*

11 *Heinrich Tessenow, design for living room in a small terrace house, c. 1916*

Note: Figs. 8 and 9 were published in Friedrich Ostendorf's *Sechs Bücher vom Bauen*, (Six Books on Architecture), Berlin, 1913.

12 *Otto Bartning, Schuster house, Wylerberg, near Cleve, 1921–4*

13 *Otto Bartning, Schuster house, Wylerberg, near Cleve, plan, 1921*

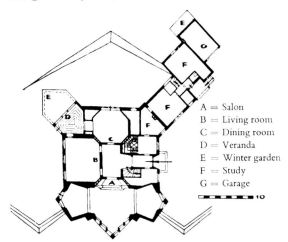

A = Salon
B = Living room
C = Dining room
D = Veranda
E = Winter garden
F = Study
G = Garage

14 *Otto Bartning, Schuster house, Wylerberg, near Cleve, 1921–4*

15 *Otto Bartning, Schuster house, Wylerberg, near Cleve, 1921–4*

2 *Elevations, plans and section, dated 14.3.36*

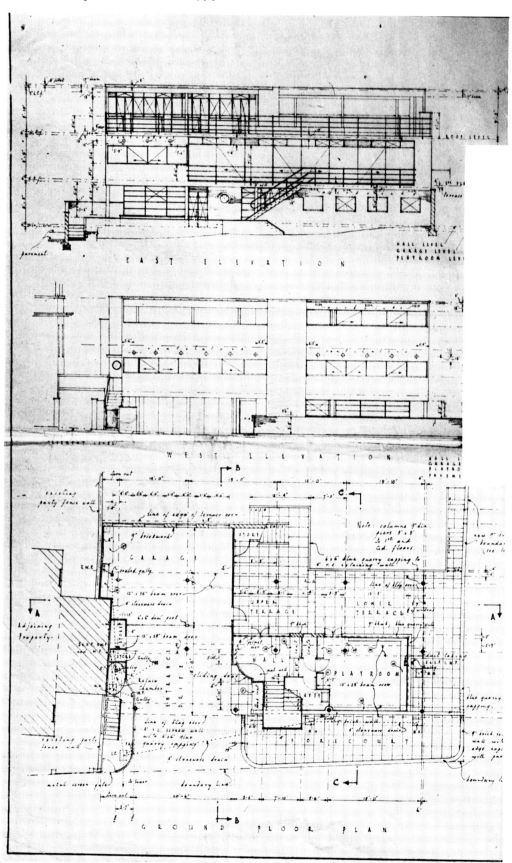

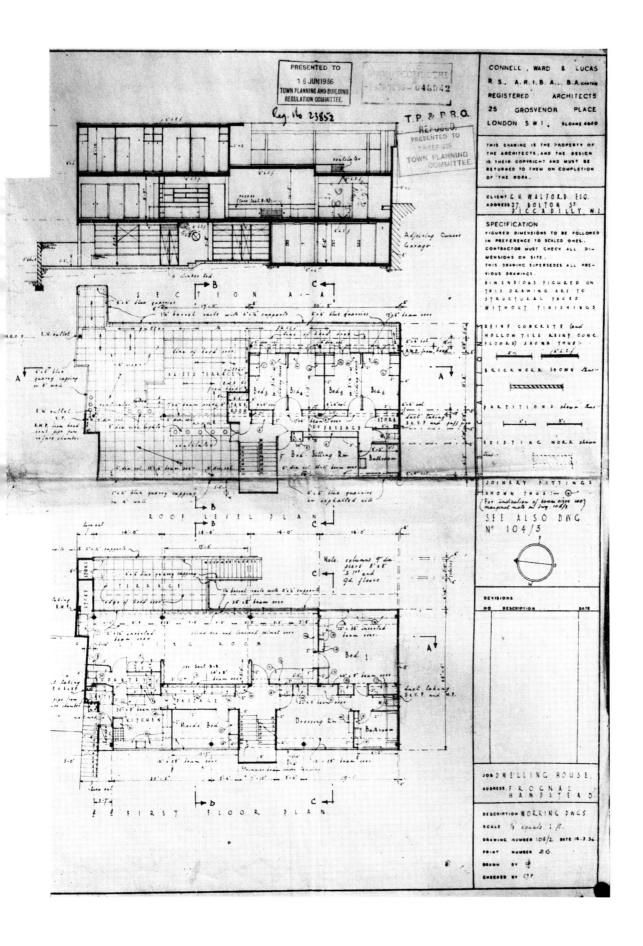

3 *Sections, elevations and plan, dated 17.3.36*

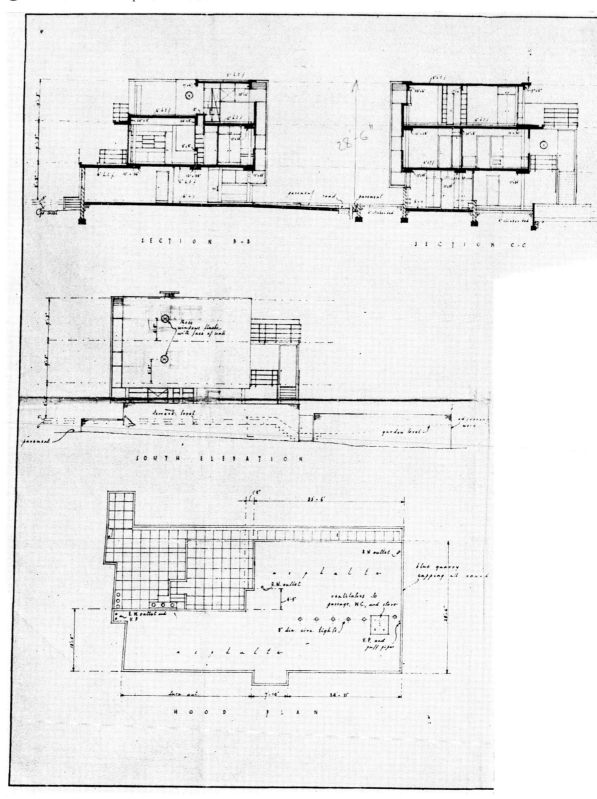

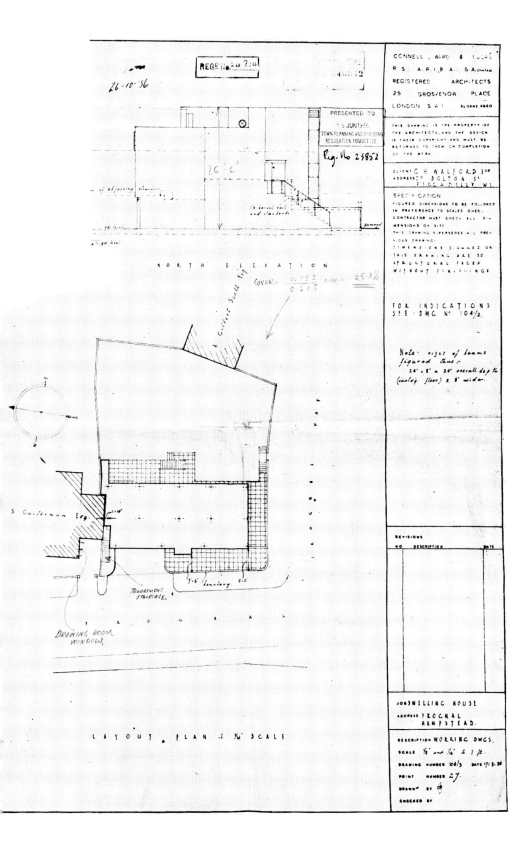

NORTH ELEVATION

LAYOUT PLAN ¼ SCALE

4 *Revised elevation of south façade*

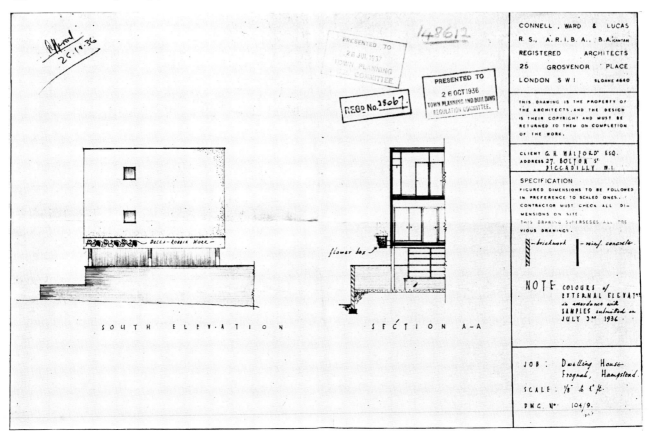

1 *The early unreformed High St Kensington station platform. It shows the jumbled confusion that Frank Pick wanted to avoid. The diamond shaped London Transport logo was one of the experimental designs used before the linear bull's-eye was finally adopted.*

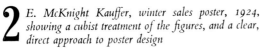

2 *E. McKnight Kauffer, winter sales poster, 1924, showing a cubist treatment of the figures, and a clear, direct approach to poster design*

3 *Fred Pegram, Burnham Beeches poster, 1923. This is a more conventional treatment than Fig. 2, and shows none of the influence of recent, continental fine art movements*

4 (*Left*) *Older Underground panel, with Grotesque lettering, unjustified type and solid bull's-eye. The general appearance of this panel is untidy and clumsy.*
(*Right*) *Newer Underground panel, using Edward Johnston's sans-serif type designed in 1916, and the linear bull's eye. This gives the appearance of being clean, neat and efficient.*

5 *F. H. Stingemore, early London Underground map designed on a geographical basis*

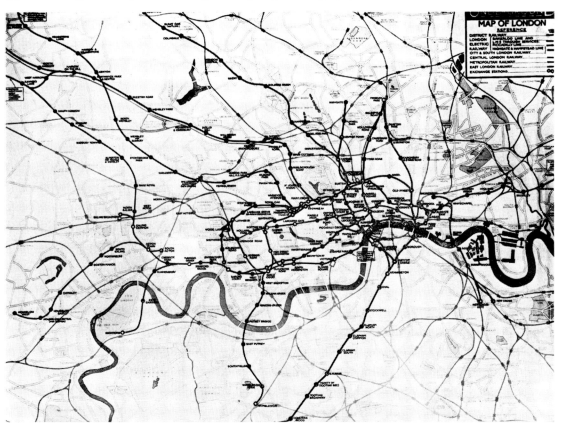

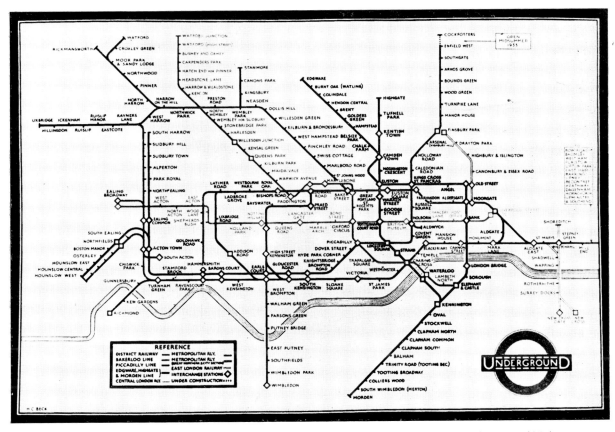

6 *Henry Beck, London Underground map designed in 1931. He has abandoned the geographical basis of Fig. 5 and used a schematic format, enlarging the central London area, and limiting the lines to horizontals, verticals and 45° angles.*

7 *Charles Holden, original architect's drawing, c. 1932, of Arnos Grove tube station on the Piccadilly line, showing the attention given to the design and placing of fixtures and fittings*

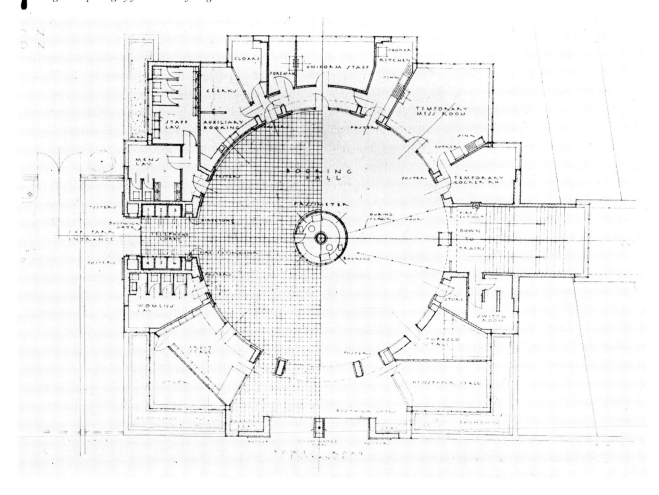

8 *Charles Holden, Oakwood station, 1932–3 (formerly Enfield West), on the Piccadilly line, showing the carefully designed litter bin, which is easy to empty. Note also the special areas for posters.*

9 *Charles Holden, Arnos Grove station platform, on the Piccadilly line, 1932–3. The dual-sided seat doubles up as a display area for the station name written on the bull's-eye logo.*

10 *Interior of rolling stock for London Underground in the late 1930s. The design is neat and unified, and the moquette has a geometric pattern using the London Transport bull's-eye motif.*

11 *Enid Marx, 'Grid' moquette 1937, designed for upholstery of seats in the Underground trains. The pattern is composed of a play of horizontals and verticals*

1 *Page from* Towards a New Architecture *by Le Corbusier*
(Etchells's translation, 1927)

2 *J. W. and M. J. Reid, Spreckles Building, San Francisco, 1897*

TOWARDS A NEW ARCHITECTURE

N.B. Let us listen to the counsels of American engineers.
But let us beware of American architects. For proof:

3 *Shreve, Lamb and Harman, Empire State Building, New York, 1931*

4 *View of 42nd St, New York, with Raymond Hood's Daily News Building centre left, and the Chrysler Building back right*

6 *Raymond Hood et al., Rockefeller Center, New York, as completed 1941*

Heights of buildings:
Empire State building: 120 storeys height: 1250 ft (or 1472 ft with aerial)
Chrysler building: 77 storeys height: 1048 ft
Daily News building: 36 storeys
Rockefeller Center Radio City tower, 70 storeys height: 850 ft

5 *Raymond Hood, Daily News Building, New York, 1930*

7 *Raymond Hood et al., Radio City, Rockefeller Center, New York, plans*

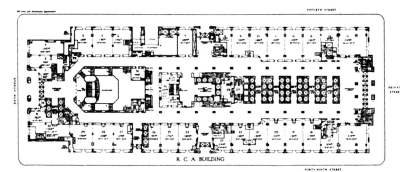

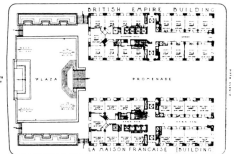

GROUND FLOOR

TWELFTH FLOOR

SIXTIETH FLOOR

9 *Hugh Ferris, 'The Four Stages,' from* The Metropolis of Tomorrow, *1929*

8 *Raymond Hood et al., Radio City, Rockefeller Center, New York, 1932*

10 *Project for the Rockefeller Center*

11 *George Howe and William Lescaze, Philadelphia Savings Fund Society (PSFS) Building, Philadelphia, 1932*

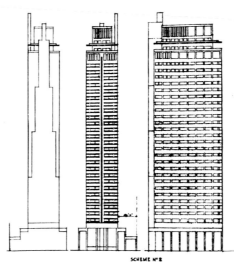

SCHEME Nº 2

13 *George Howe, project no. 2 for PSFS building (drawing dated 20.3.29)*

14 *William Lescaze, sketch for the podium of the PSFS building (drawing dated 2.12.29)*

12 *Mellor, Meigs and Howe, project for the PSFS, 1926*

15 *George Howe and William Lescaze, PSFS building*

16 *George Howe and William Lescaze, south elevation of PSFS building*

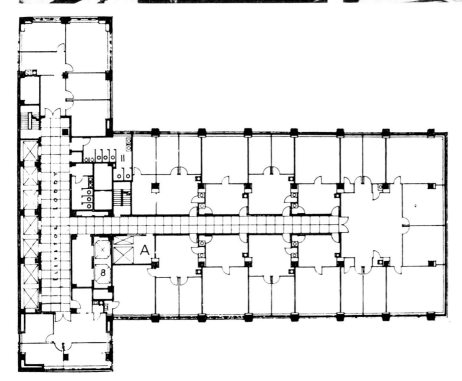

17 *Plan of PSFS showing air duct (A)*

18 *Milam building, San Antonio, Texas, 1928*

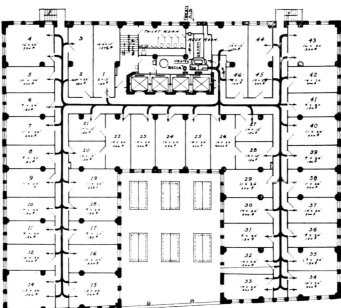

19 *George Willis, ducting for Milam building*

1 *Venesta hat-box, made in birchwood, early 1920s*

2 *Traditional furniture with beading*

3 *Jack Pritchard, block-board desk, made by Venesta, c.1930*

3a *Detail*

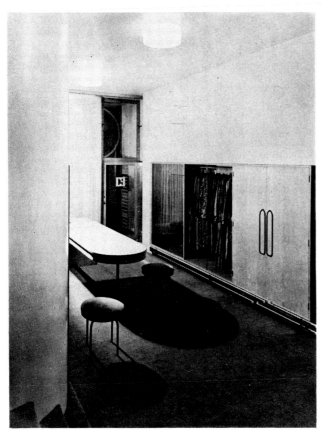

4 *Wells Coates, interior of Cresta shop, Brighton, c. 1930*

5 *Le Corbusier, Pierre Jeanneret and Charlotte Perriand, Venesta stand, London Building Trades Exhibition, 1930*

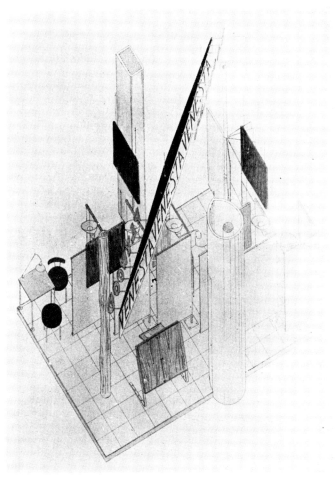

6 *Venesta stool, made by A. M. Luther & Co., Reval, 1933*

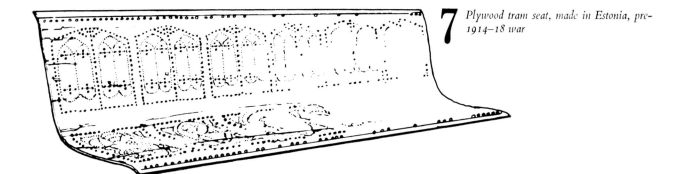

7 *Plywood tram seat, made in Estonia, pre-1914–18 war*

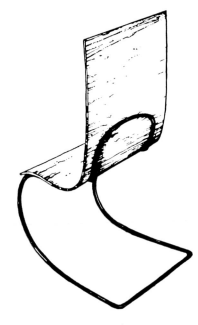

8 *Jack Pritchard, plywood chair (adapted from Fig. 7), c. 1930*

9 *Gerald Sumers, Isokon plywood trolley, c. 1933*

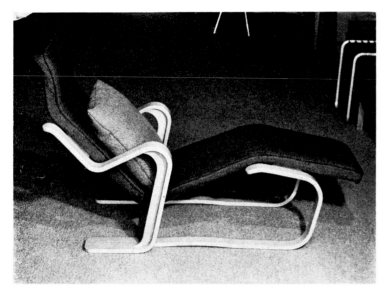

10 *Marcel Breuer, long chair, laminated birch and plywood, designed for Isokon, 1936*

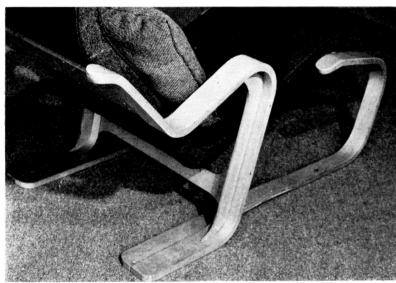

11 *Detail of vertical fin reinforcement*

12 *Marcel Breuer, plywood stacking chair, designed for Isokon, 1936*

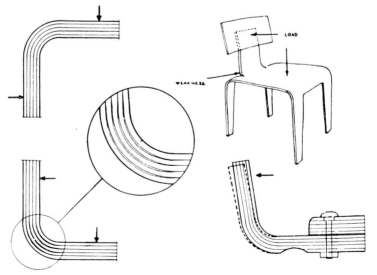

13 *Diagram to show stress points and construction problems on Breuer chair (see Fig. 12)*

14 *Arne Jacobson, plywood chair, c. 1951*

15 *Charles Eames, plywood chair, c. 1951*

16 *Egon Riess, the Isokon Penguin Donkey Mark One, 1939*

17 *Advertisement for Isokon Penguin Donkey Mark Two, redesigned by Ernest Race, c. 1964*

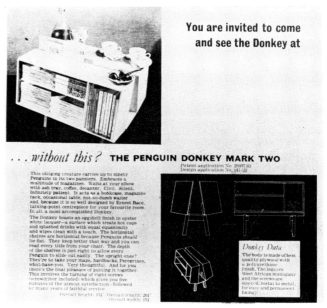

Acknowledgements

2 Magazines of Decorative Art

1 *Revue des Arts Décoratifs* 1895 p. 353   2 *L'Image* December 1896   3 *Revue des Arts Décoratifs* 1900 p. 38   4 *Cabinet Maker and Art Furnisher* September 1900 Courtesy of *Cabinet Maker*   5 Victoria & Albert Museum (Bethnal Green branch)   6 *Studio* vol 5 1894-5 Courtesy of Studio International Publications   7 *Studio* vol 19 1900 Courtesy of Studio International Publications   8 *Studio* vol 11 1897 Courtesy of Studio International Publications   9 *Art et Décoration* 1898 Courtesy of Eds. Charles Massin   10 *Art et Décoration* 1902 Courtesy of Eds. Charles Massin   11 *Jugend* vol 2 1896   12 *Pan* vol 2 1895/6   13 *Dekorative Kunst* vol 1 1897   14 *Ver Sacrum* September 1898   15 *Ver Sacrum* July 1898   16 *Ver Sacrum* July 1898   17 *Ver Sacrum* July 1898

3 Gaudí's Architecture and Design

1 to 6 Tim Benton   7 BBC   8 to 9 Tim Benton   10 J. J. Sweeney and J. L. Sert *Antonio Gaudí*, The Architectural Press, London, 1960; reprinted 1970   11 BBC   12 Tim Benton   13 BBC   14 to 16 Tim Benton   17 J. J. Sweeney and J. L. Sert *Antonio Gaudí*, The Architectural Press, London, 1960; reprinted 1970   18 BBC   19 Tim Benton   20 to 22 J. J. Sweeney and J. L. Sert *Antonio Gaudí*, The Architectural Press, London, 1960; reprinted 1970   23 BBC   24 to 25 Tim Benton

4 Hector Guimard

1 to 2 Francine Haber   3 Collection J. S. M. Scott   4 Tim Benton   5 to 6 Courtesy of the Cooper-Hewitt Museum of Decorative Arts and Design, Smithsonian Institution   7 *L'Exposition d'Art Décoratif de Copenhague 1909*, Bibliothèque Nationale   8 and 9 *Art décoratif moderne: Documents D'Atelier II 1899* Paris   8A Tim Benton   10 Collection J. S. M. Scott. Photo: Tim Benton   11 Francine Haber   12 A. Morel, editor *Entretiens sur l'Architecture Atlas* 1864, Paris   13 Tim Benton

5 Tony Garnier: La Cité Industrielle

All except 6A from Tony Garnier *Une Cité Industrielle* 1918   6A Photo: Giraudon

6 Ferro-concrete: Hennebique to Perret

1 L. G. Mouchal & Partners   2 to 7 Professor Peter Collins   8 Tim Benton   9 *L'Architecte* 1924, Courtesy of Editions Charles Massin   10 Tim Benton   11 to 12 Professor Peter Collins   13 Tim Benton   14 *La Construction Moderne* 1936 Courtesy of *La Construction Moderne*   15 to 17 Professor Peter Collins

7 Louis Sullivan

1 Hedrich-Blessing   2 Chicago Architectural Photographing Company (Henry Fuermann)   3 Chicago Architectural Photographing Company (Henry Fuermann)   4 John Szarkowski *The Idea of Louis Sullivan*, 1956, Courtesy of University of Minnesota Press   5 Chicago Historical Society Photo: Stella Jencks   6 Chicago Architectural Photographing Company (Henry Fuermann)   7 Hedrich-Blessing   8 Chicago Architectural Photographing Company (Henry Fuermann)   9 Courtesy of Art Institute of Chicago   10 Courtesy of Art Institute of Chicago

10 Futurism

1 Niedersächsisches Landesgalerie Hannover   2 Collection Paride Accetti, Milan   3 Sant'Elia Family Collection, Villa Communale dell'Olmo, Como   4 Sant'Elia Family Collection, Villa Communale dell'Olmo, Como   5 Collection Paride Accetti, Milan   6 Heinz Geretsegger and Max Peintner *Otto Wagner 1841-1918*, 1964. Courtesy of Residenz Verlag   7 Heinz Geretsegger and Max Peintner *Otto Wagner 1841-1918*, 1964. Courtesy of Residenz Verlag   8 Sant'Elia Family Collection, Villa Communale dell'Olmo, Como   9 Sant'Elia Family Collection, Villa Communale dell'Olmo, Como   10 Collection Paride Accetti, Milan   11 *Jahrbuch des Deutschen Werkbundes*, 1913   12 Sant'Elia Family Collection, Villa Communale dell'Olmo, Como   13 Tim Benton   14 Franz Masereel *The City*, 1970. Courtesy of Dover Publications Inc.

13 Monumental Architecture in the U.S.S.R.

1 Anatole Kopp *Ville et Revolution*, 1967. Courtesy of Editions Anthropos, Paris   2 to 5 Extracts from *L'Architecture Vivante* Spring 1927. Courtesy of Editions Albert Morance, Paris   6 to 7 Kirill Nikolaevich Afanas'ev *Iz istorii Sovietskaya architektura 1917-25*, 1963. Courtesy of Akademiya Nauk, Moscow   8 El Lissitsky *Russland: Die Rekonstruktion der Architektur in der Sowjetunion*, 1930. Courtesy of Verlag Anton Schroll   9 to 10 Le Corbusier *Oeuvre Complète 1910-29*. Courtesy/Artemis Verlag, Zurich   11 to 12 and 13A *Dvoretz Sovietov*, 1931/2   13 and 14 *Architectural Review* May 1932. Courtesy of Architectural Press

15 Pierre Chareau: Maison de Verre

1 to 2 Musée des Arts Décoratifs Paris. Photo: Tim Benton   3 Raymond McGrath and A. C. Frost *Glass in Architecture and Decoration*, 1937, Courtesy of Architectural Press   4 Tim Benton   5 to 6 Raymond McGrath and A. C. Frost *Glass in Architecture and Decoration*, 1937   7 and 9 to 16 Musée des Arts Décoratifs Paris. Photo: Tim Benton   8 Tim Benton   17 Lucien Hervé   18 to 27 Musée des Arts Décoratifs Paris. Photo: Tim Benton

16 Oriental Lacquer and French Design in the 1920s

1, 4 and 15 G. Janneau *Salon des Artistes Décorateurs*, 1930, Courtesy of Eds. Charles Moreau, Paris   2 *Mobilier et Décoration* 1928. Courtesy of Eds Marcel Honoré   3 Private Collection, Photo: Tim Benton   5-12 Robert Walker Collection, Paris David Amy   13-14 Photos: L. Sully Jaulmes, Paris   15 G. Janneau, *Salon des Artistes Décorateurs*, Paris, 1930, Courtesy of Eds Charles Moreau, Paris   16-17 Photos: L. Sully Jaulmes, Paris

17 Villa Savoye: Preliminary Drawings
Fondation le Corbusier, Paris. Photo: Tim Benton

19 Gordon Russell and Modern British Craftsmanship Items and illustrations Gordon Russell Ltd. Photo: David Amy   15-16 Courtesy Studio International

20 The Labour-Saving Home
1 R. Randal Phillips *Small Family Houses*, 1924. Courtesy Country Life (Hamlyn) Publications   2 R. Randal Phillips *Small Family Houses*, 1924. Courtesy Country Life (Hamlyn) Publications   3 R. Randal Phillips *Small Family Houses*, 1924. Courtesy Country Life (Hamlyn) Publications   4 to 9 Battersea Borough Council Electric House, 1927   10 R. Randal Phillips *Small Family Houses*, 1924. Courtesy Country Life (Hamlyn) Publications   11 to 13 Courtesy Architectural Press   14 Abercrombie (Sir Leslie Patrick) *The Book of the Modern House*, 1939. Courtesy Hodder & Stoughton

21 Alvar Aalto: The Failure of Total Design
1-2 Karl Fleig *Alvar Aalto* I 1963. Courtesy of Artemis Verlag und Verlag fur Architektur, Zurich   3 Museum of Finnish Architecture, Helsinki. Courtesy of Alvar Aalto   4 Courtesy of Retoria, Tokyo   5-6 Museum of Finnish Architecture, Helsinki. Courtesy of Alvar Aalto   7-8 Karl Fleig *Alvar Aalto* I, 1963. Courtesy of Artemis Verlag und Verlag fur Architektur, Zurich   9-10 Museum of Finnish Architecture, Helsinki. Courtesy of Alvar Aalto   11 Architectural Association, London. Courtesy of Miss M. Morrison   12-15 Karl Fleig *Alvar Aalto* I, 1963. Courtesy of Artemis Verlag und Verlag fur Architektur, Zurich   16 Courtesy of Retoria, Tokyo

22 Germany: The Second Tradition of the Twenties
1 *Bauwelt* 1926. Courtesy of Bertelsmann Fachzeitschriften Gmbh, Berlin   2 Nikolaus Pevsner *Europaische Architektur*, 1957. Courtesy Prestel Verlag, Berlin   3 *Wasmuths Monatshefte*, 1926. Courtesy Verlag Ernst Wasmuth, Tübingen   4-7 *Gagfah 1918-1968*, 1968. Courtesy Har-

monia Verlag Gmbh, Hamburg   8-9A Friedrich Ostendorf *Sechs Bucher vom Bauen*, 1913-20, Berlin   10-11 Heinrich Tessenow *Hausbau und dergleichen*, 1958. Courtesy Woldemar Klein Verlag Baden-Baden   12-15 Ernst Pollack *Der Baumeister Otto Bartning*, 1926. Courtesy Kurt Schroeder Verlag Königswinter   16-17 Wolfgang Pehnt *Die Architektur des Expressionismus*, 1973. Courtesy Gerd Hatje Stuttgart

23 Project Case Study: 66 Frognal Part 1
All photos Tim Benton and David Amy

24 Project Case Study: 66 Frognal Part 2
All photos BBC, courtesy Camden Borough Council

26 London Transport Design
London Transport Executive

29 The Reform of the Skyscraper
1 Courtesy Architectural Press   2 Edgar Kaufmann, Jr., editor *The Rise of an American Architecture*, 1970. Courtesy The Pall Mall Press   3 Helmsley-Spear Inc.   4 Reprinted with permission from *Architectural Record*, March 1933   5 New York Public Library   6 *Architectural Review*, December 1950. Courtesy of Rockefeller Center Inc. Photo: Thomas Airviews   7 Courtesy Dr. Winston R. Weisman   8 *Architectural Forum*, October 1933   9 Courtesy Mrs. Hugh Ferriss   10 Courtesy Mrs. Hugh Ferriss   11 to 13 Courtesy of *Journal of the Society of Architectural Historians*   14 Courtesy of Lescaze Family   15 to 16 Courtesy of *Journal of the Society of Architectural Historians*   17 to 19 Reyner Banham *The Architecture of the Well-Tempered Environment*, 1969. Courtesy of Architectural Press

30 The Work of Isokon
1 BBC   2 Jack Pritchard   3 and 3A BBC   4 Courtesy Mrs. Laura Cohn   5 Jack Pritchard   6 BBC   7 to 9 Jack Pritchard   10 to 12 BBC   13 Jack Pritchard   14 A. Greave. Photo: BBC   15 BBC   16 to 17 Jack Pritchard